WHEN
AM I
READY?

KINGSLEY OKONKWO

TABLE OF CONTENT

ACKNOWLEDGEMENT

Many have invested their time and energies into producing this book you have in your hand and should be duly appreciated.

I'd like to thank God for the call, the grace and ability to do His will at all times.

All those who worked on the book especially Pastor Peter Emeaghara and his wonderful team of proofreaders – you know who you are.

Base media: Thank you, you've been a great help.

My Pastor, Reverend 'Femi Albert Oduwole, for all your encouragement, you helped stir up the gift in me. Thank you sir.

And of course, to my beautiful wife, Mildred. I don't think there are enough words to describe the impact you have had on my life and ministry – I love you.

And finally, to all those who have attended our relationship meetings over the years. Without the inspiration of the Holy Spirit and your audience, I would not have preached this message that has become this powerful book.

FOREWORD

I love to say, "There is no institution where marriage is taught, yet marriage is the only institution where you get the certificate, before you start the learning process".

How true that is. There was never a time all through my years of learning that I got to class and one of the tutors said, "today we are studying marriage 101 or wifery 205".

The only thing we were taught was husbandry, but alas it was animal husbandry (no wonder some husbands behave like animals).

This is why it is expedient that men of God, full of insight write books on this all-important subject of marriage. Marriage is meant to be a haven, not an oven, and it is meant to be for bliss not for blisters. For this to be, principles must be put in motion.

When a man has a physical malady, he sees a doctor who examines him, but if it is a real malady, like an emotional or spiritual problem, Apostle Paul said," let every man examine himself," (1 Corinthians 11:28)

This shows that, I can not examine you for you, especially when it comes to your readiness for marriage. This is why I highly recommend this book written by a man of this generation in a language that this generation understands. After reading this book, you will stop asking, "AM I READY?" And you will be able to examine yourself to know if you are or not. Every Pastor, parent and counsellor who has problems answering this question should read this book and also recommend it for others because it is full of revelation and practical insights.
Stay hooked to the power source.

ALBERT FEMI ODUWOLE
WORD ABLAZE MINISTRIES
INTERNATIONAL, IBADAN.

PREFACE

I have been teaching singles about relationships and courtship for some years now. I have travelled extensively preaching on campuses and in seminars to many singles and I have discovered that one of the most common question people ask about marriage and courtship is "when am I ready"?

This intriguing question has inspired me to write this book. In the next few chapters, these questions will be answered, as well as others such as:
What are the signs to look out for in order to know when I am ready?
What must I attain, achieve and acquire to be considered ready?
What are the things to look out for in a partner?
And many more!

This book will not only help you recognize when you are ready for courtship or marriage, it will also help you discern if your partner to be is ready as well because for

marriage to be successful, both parties must be ready. This book is written to inspire and prepare you for a blissful marriage as it answers the question,
"WHEN AM I READY?"

CHAPTER ONE

ARE YOU READY?

28 "For *which of you, intending to build a tower,*
sitteth not down first, and counteth the cost
whether he has sufficient to finish it?
29Lest haply, after he has laid the foundation,
and is not able to finish it; all that behold him,
begin to mock him,
30Saying, This man began to build, and was not
able to finish."

- Luke 14: 28-30

Today, divorces, broken homes, extra-marital affairs, or couples living together, pretending to be happy are the order of the day. Some of us don't even have to look beyond our own homes to see these situations.

It is indeed sad that most of the marriages we see around us are just a shadow of what marriage was intended to be. Some of us even have our parents' marriage as an example of the sorry state marriages are in today. This is the major reason we must prepare ourselves adequately before getting involved in relationships and marriage.

A lot of people have entered into courtships or even marriages without being prepared for it and as such have had a hard time that they end up breaking up. Sometimes, the reverse is the case as some people have been ready for relationships but were neither aware that the time was right for them to start looking out for the right person nor how to position themselves to be found and have still remained single.

HOW DO YOU KNOW WHEN YOU ARE READY?

The scripture above shows us that it is not enough to desire to build, it is even more important to sit down and figure out how much it will cost, so you will know if you have enough to complete the building. If you relate this scripture to marriage, it is simply saying that, it is not sufficient to desire to get married. you must first sit down to count the cost to see if you have what it takes to make it work and last a life time.

The height of a building is determined by its' foundation. If an architect were to pass by a construction site, by merely looking at the foundation, he can tell whether it will be a bungalow or a mansion. The foundation determines the strength of the building; the Bible says in Psalm 11: 3 [NKJV],

"If the foundation be faulty, what can the righteous do?"

Nobody would dare build a tower without first counting the cost or laying proper foundation and just as the size and height of a building is determined and sustained by its foundation, likewise, your preparedness will determine how good your marriage will be and how long it will last.

COUNT THE COST

If you are planning for a marriage that will span five to ten years, then you can rush into it without being adequately prepared. But if your focus is a marriage that will last a lifetime, you must plan and prepare for it properly. And just as every building need its own foundation built in its own peculiar style, marriages are also different from each other. Therefore, you must not compare yourself with other people. Don't apply standards or methods that are not scriptural to your life.

Irrespective of what others have said or done, count the cost, then ask yourself honestly,
"Do I have what it takes to make it work?"
"Do I have what it takes to make it last?"
You must ask yourself genuinely "Am I ready?"

I know you might be saying, "Pastor Kinsley, you don't know how old I am, time is running out". Sweetheart, if you waited this long, it makes sense to do it right. Age should not be the major reason to think you are ready for marriage. The truth is, marriage is not all about you. Will your spouse be fulfilled? Will you be a good parent? Will you have a godly influence on your children? Age alone doesn't make you ready. There are a whole lot of other issues involved.

The Bible tells us, "...and the two shall become one flesh." This implies that in God's math, one plus one equals one. The necessary question that should arise here is, "if they are equal to one, doesn't it then mean that they were two halves?" The answer is simply this, according to God's word, if each party is a half and not whole, if they come together they will still remain halves. Both parties- man and woman must be whole and ready, to become one.

Being ready doesn't just mean physical maturity. Take a fruit for instance, just because a fruit is big and fully grown in size, does not necessarily mean it is ripe or ready for consumption. An unripe mango for instance, can be one of the worst things one can ever eat. It is acidic and can be detrimental to ones' health. It can be compared to getting married to a partner who is not ready. If the person is not 'ripe' for marriage, though (s)he may look physically mature, it could be disastrous to go ahead with the marriage.

I have discovered over the years that one of the major complaints people approach me with is that of an individual turning them down when they propose to them. I try to make them understand that the person may not be ripe (ready) for marriage and should be left alone until (s)he is ready (of course this is not the only reason). Just as the analogy of the big and unripe fruit earlier mentioned, it will take a lot of energy to dislodge the fruit from the tree even when constantly hitting it. However, with a ripe fruit, the reverse is the case. You barely need to tap the fruit before it comes tumbling down. This is no different from a person who is prepared for marriage.

BE THE RIGHT PERSON

Another question I am constantly confronted with is, "How do I find the right person?" It is amazing how people constantly miss the major issue when it comes to finding a life partner. The priority should be in being the right person. You need to be the right person first, before you can find the right person. It is only when you are the right person that you will have the ability to recognize and appreciate the right person when (s) he comes along.

Being ready also involves brokenness. Many people are arrogant, self righteous and conceited. They may be mature physically and intellectually but they are not ready for marriage. They think that they have a degree and are physically mature, they have the right to make endless list of preposterous qualities that they require in a partner and in most cases they lack in themselves. The next six chapters will help prepare you for marriage.

CHAPTER TWO

WHAT IS YOUR PERSPECTIVE?

"For as a man thinks in his heart so is he".
- Proverbs 23: 7a

The perspective you have concerning anything determines your general attitude towards that thing. For instance, your perspective towards life determines your attitude towards life. It is also true that your perspective of God determines your attitude towards God. You must also understand that your attitude determines what you get from anything.

We can then deduce from the principle above, that perspective determines attitude, and attitude determines outcome. If we apply this principle to the issue of marriage, it simply implies that your perspective of marriage will determine your attitude towards marriage and determine the outcome or what you get out of it.

The Oxford Advance Learner's dictionary defines perspective as, "a particular attitude towards something or a point of view". Our attitudes are usually based on or influenced by past experiences, culture or back ground.

The first area to tackle in getting ready for marriage is your perspective towards marriage. What are the things you have seen or heard that has coloured your perspective? It is important that you establish what your perspective is as this determines the outcome of your marriage. If you are planning to get married, you must first understand marriage from the perspective of its originator. Your perspective must be governed by His. For example, in the kingdom of God where we operate, relationships are considered sacred. This means that we are not allowed to dabble into all sorts of unholy activities under the pretext of dating. In this kingdom, we don't talk about having boyfriends and girlfriends simply because the Bible which is our manual does not refer to courtship union as that of boyfriend and girlfriend but a man and wife. Christian men looking for life partners don't find themselves girls, chicks or babes as they are more often called but wives. The bible makes it clear in the following scriptures:

"Therefore shall a MAN leave his father and mother, and shall cleave to his WIFE: and they shall be one flesh."

-Genesis 2:24

"Whoso findeth a WIFE, findeth a good thing..."

-Proverb 18:22

"And said for this cause shall a MAN leave father and mother, and shall cleave to his WIFE; and they twain shall be one flesh."

-Matthew 19:5

In today's world, it is normal for people to change partners like a lady trying on clothes in a boutique. It has become the norm for people to get in and out of relationships as they desire even if it is just for the fun of it. However, this is not acceptable in the kingdom of God. In this kingdom, relationships are given the highest level of regards and you are only permitted to get into it if you are seriously thinking of getting married. No other reason is permissible.

The importance of having the right perspective can never be over- emphasized. The Bible makes it clear that a man's perspective which is the same as his imaginations, his thought pattern or how he view things determines his attitude and expectation and these go a long way in determining what he gets out of life.

"….and now nothing will be restrained from them; which they have IMAGINED to do."
-Genesis 1: 6

"For surely there is an end; and thine EXPECTATION
shall not be cut off."
-Proverbs 23:18

"And be not conformed to this world; but be ye transformed by the renewing of your MIND(thought pattern), that ye may prove

what is that good, and acceptable, and
perfect will of God."   - *Romans 1:2*

From these scripture references, it is clear
that having the right perspective is
important. For instance, someone who
believes that fighting in marriage is natural
and does not correct that wrong perspective
before getting married will naturally have a
hard time in marriage and end up fighting
their spouse all the time. Infact, I once
counselled a lady who told me that she
believed that she and her husband will fight
but that it will draw them closer when they
made up. She said this emphatically
believing it was normal. This is such a
wrong perspective, as she believes that for
them to attain a great level of intimacy in
marriage, they would have to fight
regularly. If you think like that, your
wedding gift from me would be a first aid
box.

Another lady told me that she believed that
her husband would commit adultery but she
would not be perturbed, since she knew that
it was a common and natural occurrence

with married men. She would be content with the fact that she knows how to lure him home to her and that she is his legal wife and not a mistress.

These perspectives, which rather unscriptural, if not corrected before marriage, can lead to a frustrating time in marriage.

Sometimes, these perspectives which are usually unscriptural comes from the things we hear our parents say or do. For instance, it is very common for some mothers to fill their daughters head with statements like, "All men are the same. Don't trust any man." My response to this is simply this: "how come you got married to one?" we cannot make a sweeping statement based on someone's negative experience.

Men are not exempt from expressions like these.

The common one is, "women are useless, and all they are after is your money, never love a woman." My response to that is no different. It is important that we do not let other people's negative experiences becloud our perspectives.

It is also very common to see a lot of unhappy homes today, where children are brought up in an environment where they live with a father who thinks he is 'Mike Tyson', and constantly uses their mother or even sometimes the children themselves as the punching bags. They therefore grow up to think that marriage is not worth the trouble. This is a wrong perspective. I want you to know that no matter how bad your parents' union was or is, you should not let it becloud your perspective or it will destroy your life. Even if you were in a relationship that ended badly, don't let it colour your perspective concerning marriage. I want to remind you that the word of God is more powerful than any negative experience you have ever had. No experience can ever change the word of God.

You must remember that God is the originator of marriage and His perspective on marriage is…

"Two are better than one; because they shall

have good reward for their labour."

-Ecclesiastes 4:9

"One shall chase a thousand,two shall chase ten thousand."

Multiplied impact! Amazing! When two prepared individuals come together, they maximize their potentials and the result is usually breathtaking.

"Whoso findeth a wife findeth a good thing and obtains favour of the Lord."

- Proverbs 18:22

According to God, marriage is a good thing. He created marriage and the Bible tells us that, as all other things he created, to him it was very good. He also declared that when you get married, an uncommon level of favour would follow you.

Contrary to what most Christians believe, the scripture reference above is not a prayer point, but simply the natural other that things should follow when you get married in accordance with God's word. The power of that scripture is not in how many hours you spend in sending it back to him in prayers, but in the dept of understanding that you have of it. God is saying to us that marriage is a good thing as it yields the combined favour of two.

"...it is not good that the man should be alone; I will make him a helpmeet for him."
-Genesis 2:18
"Marriage is honourable in all ..."
-Hebrews 13: 4

Marriage is celebrated and encouraged everywhere in the Bible. It is not a man's idea. It did not start with your parents or forefathers, neither is it your church doctrine nor pastor's idea. Marriage was originated by God. He initiated the first marriage, which was between Adam and Eve. Adam never asked God for a wife. He didn't even realize that he needed one. Adam was just going about his business as usual. It was God who initiated the union. He knew that Adam needed someone of his kind to communicate with, someone to multiply his efforts, to challenge his potentials to bring out the best in him. So God gave him Eve as his wife. Since God gave him a wife, it shows that she was a gift and marriage is a gift from God. The Bible goes on to tell us that, "every good and perfect gift comes from God..." (James 1:17). If marriage is from God, then it is good and perfect.

IS A PERFECT MARRIAGE POSSIBLE?
For as long as I can remember, I've heard people say that you must have problems in marriage.

Honestly, I'm tired of hearing it. I believe that God is a good God and as part of his plan, he always prepares us for any eventualities that we may come across. For instance, before he left he said, "In this world you will have tribulations..." he also said, "Men will persecute you for the gospel's sake." And that we have seen all around us. Do you then think that God who cares so much about us would not have informed us that there are supposed to be fights in marriage. He holds the manual.

He would have told us you are to fight, break up, settle, come back together then fight again and so on. But he never did.

I understand that you can face external challenges e.g. financial difficulties, illness (which you can still have victory over) but not internal challenges. Even if you are from different back grounds and different cultures, as people claim, that is not enough reason for problems in marriage.

There is only one Bible, so if we line up with it no matter where we are coming from, it erases the effect of our different cultures or backgrounds and gives us one perspective and we become one. My wife and I had the same perspective based on the word of God that really helped us.

On thing you must realize is that a perfect marriage is possible. This is the perspective you should have concerning marriage. Contrary to what you may believe, a perfect marriage does not mean that both parties will not occasionally see things differently; after all human beings are different. It simply means that even when that happens, they will choose not to quarrel or trade punches over the issue. You don't have to be 100% like your partner for marriage to be perfect. Infact renowned writer and family therapist Tim Lahaye argues that opposite attract. Couples have to decide and choose to agree or find a meeting point regardless of their differences and have a quarrel free and stress free union. God says a perfect marriage is possible, so, it is.

The late Kenneth E. Hagin for instance, was married for over 60 years and it was not a trial and error situation. He and his wife were aware that marriage was to be a life time affair, so before they got married, they made a vow to each other to remain sweethearts till the very end. No fights, no quarrels, no malice. They promised to love each other forever, and they were committed to it. Whenever Kenneth Hagin was in town and not away on preaching engagement, he will bring his wife breakfast in bed. They would share a kiss before every meal and he would help with the dishes. This he did for 60 or more years.

Bishop David Oyedepo has had a testimony of a quarrel-free and stress-free marriage for over 25years now. He told the story of when he and his wife was still in courtship, an elderly Christian, a highly respected man and a spiritual father to his fiancée, while counselling them asked him, "David, what are you looking forward to in marriage?"

Bishop Oyedepo answered, "I am looking forward to a stress-free marriage." The old man laughed and said, "That's not possible, you cannot have a stress-free marriage."
"But we have been in courtship for a while now and we have not had the first quarrel" Bishop Oyedepo replied. The elderly man smiled and said ," That's courtship, the two parties are apart but in marriage they are close together, and it is not possible for two people to be together and not step on each others toes."

"But sir," Bishop Oyedepo answered, "I am sitting next to you and we are very close, why am I not stepping on your toes?"

The elderly man was quiet and Bishop Oyedepo continued, "two reasons: one, I am not blind, I can see your toes. Two, I am not wicked. I can't see your toes and step on them intentionally."

That put an end to the conversation. He had the right perspective from the outset and this has reflected on his marriage years later. A perfect marriage is possible but it is important to have the right perspective. Align your perspective with God's word. If both parties have the right perspective, that is in alignment with God's word and are committed to playing their parts, there will be no problem in marriage.

Thank God, my wife has this same perspective. It has been the secret to our quarrel-free courtship and marriage. We don't fight about anything. We made up our mind from the beginning that it had to be God's way. It takes two to quarrel. Fights don't start suddenly; there's always a gradual build –up. You can decide to walk in love.

The key is in knowing God's word and obeying it. His wisdom cannot fail. You cannot know more about a thing than its creator. So if God who created marriage says that a perfect marriage is possible, then settle it once and for all in your heart that it is!!!

CHAPTER THREE

ARE YOU INFORMED?

"My people are destroyed for lack of knowledge. Because you have rejected knowledge, I will also reject you."
                              - Hosea 4:6[NKJV]

The Bible tells us quite clearly that people fail because they lack information about what they do. You must get informed before you get involved. Don't get involved with anyone before you get informed about relationships and marriage. Information must come before involvement or else you are heading for failure or even destruction.

Luke 6: 47-48 states,

47 *"Whosoever cometh to me, and heareth my sayings, and doeth them, I will shew you to whom he is like;*
48 He is like a man which built an house and digged deep, and laid the foundation on a rock: and when the flood arose, the stream beat vehemently upon that house and could not shake it: for it was founded upon a rock".

The Bible tells us that the wind could not shake the house because the builder dug deep- he sought and acquired adequate information and with that information, he laid a firm foundation upon which he built the house. If you want a marriage that is built to last, then you must get all the information possible on how to build one. You cannot afford to leave it to the last minute. You must get all the information you need no mater the cost, before you start building.

It takes a medical doctor about six to seven years to acquire the necessary knowledge information he will need to become qualified. We never allow anyone with any less experience treat us when we are ill. Isn't it amazing then, that we get married to people who are ignorant about marriage, or choose as our life partners people who have absolutely no information about something we will spend the rest of our lives doing. Marriage require no less from you than the same dedication with which you would pursue a career, considering the fact that one is not expected to resign from marriage as one would a job, if it's not working out. You need to prepare yourself. Read books, attend seminars on courtship and marriage and most importantly search the bible for relevant information. Lay a good foundation for your future. Lack of information will only result in frustration especially since you and your partner are likely to be different from each other.

DIFFERENCES BETWEEN MEN AND WOMEN

The truth is, the average person does not know that there are differences between a man and a woman. First of all men and women do not think alike. It is wrong to expect a woman to think like a man or a man like a woman. As a man don't just assume that a woman thinks and reasons through everything looking for a logical explanation like you do. While as a woman, don't presuppose that a man has any hidden implication behind the things he says to you. Men usually just say what they mean, while you have to decode what a woman means from what she says. For instance, if a woman says, "you don't love me anymore" she simply means that she is not feeling loved at that time or that you have not been saying those three magic words often enough.

Women to a large extent are emotional beings, while men are basically logical beings. Women are feelers- they are intuitive, while men on the other hand are thinkers-they reason out things most times, trying to find logical explanations for everything.

Women speak for relational purposes. They speak to show affection. A woman engages in a discussion because she likes the person and wants to enjoy the companionship. Men on the other hand, speak to pass across information. He engages in a discussion to get facts.

Women like to be complimented. If a woman asks your opinion about the dress she is wearing, she is not necessarily asking for your analysis of what she is wearing but an approval of it. Men alternatively when they ask your opinion of anything usually want analysis of the subject.

Women are motivated by what they hear, which is why compliment works with women most of the time. Even poems that a man may find silly may just be absolutely fantastic to a woman and score you many good points with her. In contrast, men are moved by what they see. When a man gets married he expects that his wife will retain the beauty that attracted him to her in the first place. If she starts to loose interest in her physical appearance and personal hygiene, he tends to be dispirited and begin to wonder if he made the right choice. Every normal man irrespective of his age is moved by what he sees.

Ladies, let me take some time to talk to you. Just because you are now married or have stared having children should not stop you from looking your best or from taking care of yourself. You must remain attractive to your husband. Remember men are moved largely by what they see. You must take the time to prepare for your husband everyday; take an evening bath, wear sexy lingerie, a sweet fragrance, and put on light make up if you need to. Your focus should be to enhance your beauty generally.

Look at it this way, your husband wakes up with you everyday, sees you looking pale, gawky, unkempt in the morning, then goes off to work and he probably works in a company where he is bound to see well dressed, sweet smelling, and articulate, stylish ladies with poise. Everyday he is faced with the unfortunate task of having to compare these attractive ladies at work with the unattractive wife he left in the morning and will still meet at home. Do not make it easy for your husband to be tempted. Please take care of yourselves. Always look good for him. Even if he is spirit filled, remember that men are moved by what they see.

Frederick K.C Price once shared the story of a woman who approached him requesting for prayers for her husband because their marriage is heading for trouble. Out of the concern he had for her, he wanted to pray for her but instead, he felt led to visit her home. When he got there, while looking around, a picture caught his attention. In the picture were a young man and his beautiful bride.

He asked the woman, "Who are these people in this picture?" she replied "my husband and I". K.C. Price was stunned by her reply. He could not believe his eyes. The woman standing beside him was a huge contrast with the woman in the picture. She had put on so much weight that she had now become obese. He said to her, "your husband does not have a problem. You have taken away his real wife. Give him back the woman he married. You are so different from the woman in the picture that's why he is acting strangely towards you. Give him back his real wife."

This applies to the men as well. Just because a woman is largely moved by what she hears doesn't mean that she is not moved AT ALL by what she sees. Don't let yourself go. It is very common for a slim man with an athletic build, after a few years, to become so fat with a potbelly that makes it nearly impossible for him to see his feet. He then expects that his wife will remain attracted to him and will be eager to see him at the end of the day.

For women, words are very powerful. It can either make or mar their personality, which is why a man should avoid calling his wife names, ordering her around and speaking unpleasant words to her. You hold the key to building or destroying her self-esteem, so even when correcting her, address the issues, don't attack her person. Always use pleasant and appreciative words and you will be pleasantly surprised at the positive impact it will have on her.

It is often said that one of the ways to a man's heart is through his stomach. It is therefore very important that every woman that is preparing to settle down should know how to cook. Every man wants to come home to a good home cooked meal and anywhere a man finds good food he will return there regularly.

These are just few of the differences both parties should be acquainted with before getting involved to ensure that they do not frustrate each other in marriage. However, apart from the differences and needs of men and women, there are some things that will be peculiar to your partner. It is your personal responsibility to find them out either by asking or by paying close attention to your partner. This is precisely the purpose of courtship.

COURTSHIP: A TIME FOR INTERVIEW NOT INTERCOURSE.

Courtship is the period from the moment you both agreed to get married till the time you are actually joined together as man and wife. It is the time when you and your partner are expected to get to know each other better. It's a time to plan and not to play. Courtship is like a dress rehearsal for marriage. The intimacy-not intercourse- you developed during this period will go a long way in sustaining your marriage.

This is the time to be very observant because if you notice anything in your partner that you cannot live with or that you feel will pose a problem to the union; this is the time to deal with it. Even if you have to break it up, remember a broken courtship is better than a broken marriage. Courtship is the time to learn all you possibly can learn about your partner and your roles in marriage.

KNOW YOUR ROLES.
It is important that you know and understand your respective roles in marriage before getting involved.

THE WOMAN
22Wives submit yourselves unto your own husbands, as unto the Lord.

23 For the husband is the head of the wife, even as Christ is the head of the church and he is the saviour of the body.
24 Therefore as the church is subject unto Christ, so let the wives be to their own husbands in everything.

-Ephesians 5:22-24

According to Gods word, the principal role of a woman in marriage is submission. The Bible says that you are to submit in everything. Your role is SUBMITSSION not DISCUSSION. God did not ask you to confront and demand your right from him. Some women believe they know more than their husbands and want to control him. They are indirectly saying they know more than God. If God says the man is the head, accept it and cooperate with him. Even when there is a slight difference in age, or the woman is even older than the man, she must still submit. God did not say the older, richer, or wiser, of the two is the head. His word is clear. The man is the head. So before you agree to marry any man, the question you should ask yourself is," can I submit to him in everything? Do I really respect him?" respect is a major need of men.

Don't think that God is unfair in asking you to submit to the man in everything. He gave you the first right in marriage, which is the right to choose. You get to choose who you submit to. So choose wisely.

THE MAN

25 Husbands, LOVE your wives, even as Christ also loved the church, and gave himself for it;
28 So ought men to LOVE their wives as their own bodies. He that loveth his wife loveth himself.

- Ephesians 5:25&28

The man's principal role in marriage is to love his wife, even as Christ loves the church. You as the man must love her enough to sacrifice anything for her. Apart from God you should not put anything before her; not your family, friends, job or even ministry. Love her like you love yourself.

Some men are chauvinistic. They place no value on women. They see them as objects for satisfying their desires. They bully ladies and insist on always having their way. As a single man, if you cannot love and treat the ladies in your life-your mother, sisters and friends with respect, you won't have the ability to love and respect your wife the way you should. You must understand that respect is earned not demanded. Just because you are always shouting, "I am the head" or "I am the man" doesn't mean you will earn her respect. Treat her right and you will earn her respect.

Consider doing what the Bible says in 1 peter 3:7, "Treat your wife (or wife- to- be) according to knowledge, giving honour unto her as unto the weaker vessel". Now when the bible describes her as the weaker vessel, it doesn't mean that she is less than the man but that she is merely more fragile and should be handled with care before and after the wedding.

THE WEDDING IS NOT THE MARRIAGE

The wedding and the marriage are two different things. The day both parties are joined as man and wife is the wedding, while the marriage begins after the wedding. The wedding lasts for just a couple of hours while the marriage is meant to last a lifetime.

Most people would do anything to have a flamboyant wedding. They invest millions in the wedding and make absolutely no investments in the marriage. They spend outrageous amounts of money to make sure they come up with unique invitation cards, perfect hall decorations, the best caterers, photographers, make-up artist and the like.
They rent limousines and luxury cars to convey them to the wedding. The clothes and accessories are imported from all sorts of exotic places and of course the wedding is given so much coverage that it is in all the magazines and television stations possible. All these are done for a wedding that will last for just one day.

However, if you are to ask these same people how much they have invested in the marriage itself, or how informed they are about marriage and each persons role in the marriage; they would just stare at you looking confused. They have invested absolutely nothing! They haven't listened to a single tape, read any book, or attended any seminar on courtship and marriage. And they expect their marriage to work out like magic. They spend millions of money on the wedding and not a single dime on the marriage .This is so terrible.

People spend so much on weddings because they are trying to please everyone. Some even have wedding ceremonies that are so large that at the end of the day, they are either broke or in debt. The funny thing is the flamboyance of the wedding does not guarantee a good marriage. Do not allow anyone pressurize you into having a wedding ceremony you cannot afford. The ceremony is not as important as the long-term commitment. Invest in knowledge. Read books, listen to tapes, and attend seminars on marriage and courtship. I mean don't just borrow tapes and books; build a personal library that you can refer to from time to time. Dig deep, build a solid foundation for marital bliss. Remember it is important to get informed before getting involved.

CHAPTER FOUR

ARE YOU MATURE?

"When I was a child, I spake as a child, I thought as a child: but when I became a man, I put away childish things"
                        - 1 Corinthians 13: 11

A lot of people have tried to differentiate between age and maturity and I particularly like the saying that,

"Ageing is growing old, while maturity is growing up".

It just sums it up perfectly. It has also been said that you can only be young for a period of time, but you can be immature for life.

Maturity has never and will never be a function of age. It is a function of wisdom, responsibility and exposure. It is quite common to see many immature old men who are still as confused today as they were twenty years ago and in contrast, young, intelligent, responsible people, who at their age exhibit a strong sense of direction.

Over time as a pastor, I have come to realize that a great marriage is never between two perfect but mature people. No one is perfect but you can be mature. When the bible talks about being perfect, it is simply referring to maturity. It means to be balanced and have control. Marriage is for matured men and women and not for boys and girls.

4 *"And he answered and said unto them, have you not read that He which made them at the beginning made them male and female.*

5 And said, for this cause shall a man leave his father and mother, and shall cleave to his wife; And they twain shall be one flesh?"
-Matthew 19: 4-5

Verse 5 in the scripture above says, a man (not a boy) will leave and cleave to his wife; a woman (not a girl). Age is not the sole determining factor whether one is a man or woman. Rather, maturity is the determinant. And as I said earlier, maturity is a function of wisdom, responsibility and exposure.

Being male or female is a matter of chance; becoming a man or woman is a matter of choice. Verse 4 of the earlier mentioned scripture says *"He who made them at the beginning made them male and female."* This implies that being male or female is a matter of chance. God, not you made that decision. However, becoming a man or a woman; becoming mature is your choice. That is why Paul said in 1 Corinthians 13: 11,

"When I was a child (either male or female) I spake as a child, I thought as a child: but when I become a man (grew up to maturity) I put away childish things."

Maturity is your responsibility. It is your responsibility to put away childish things and grow up to maturity. Marriage is not for children but for grown ups. It is for mature people. So until you are mature you are not ready for marriage.

FOUR SIGNIFICANT WORDS THAT REVEALS MATURITY.

Maturity is not something that can be hidden. It is part of a person's character and thus is evident for all to see in a person's life. We will take a look at four words that reflects maturity in an individual's life. The first word we will be addressing is

NO.
"...But let your yes be yes; and your no; no; lest you fall into condemnation."

This is one of the easiest ways to determine one who is immature. An immature person hardly says no to anything and is easily influenced by friends and people around. (S)he doesn't have a mind of his/her own and finds it hard to say no even to the things (s)he doesn't really want.

One of the things you must learn as a mature person is how to say no. For one, you must never compromise your stand as a Christian. Avoid places and people that can ruin your reputation. Saying no to the things that can hinder or destroy your life is a major trait of maturity. It is one of the major ways of differentiating between a child and a man. A child hardly ever says no especially to the things (s) he enjoys doing even if it is bad for him/her. When a child is asked:
"Do you want ice cream?" (s)he says "yes".
"Do you want biscuits?" "Yes"
"Do you want to play" "yes"
That is the typical manner in which a child speaks. A mature person on the other hand, knows how and when to say no.

"...Moses, when he had grown to maturity REFUSED to be called the son of Pharaoh's daughter".
-Hebrews 11:24

When Moses had reached a stage of maturity he learned to say no to being called the son of Pharaoh's daughter. His saying no had a lot of implications but he was ready as a matured person to take the consequences. It will have been much easier for him to still be referred to as Pharaohs grandson but that's where maturity comes in. It doesn't compromise.

As singles, you will face a lot of sexual temptation. Your ability to say no to premarital sex is proof that you are mature. Many have enjoyed a moment's pleasure that had long-term consequences that ranges from unwanted pregnancies, to sexually transmitted deceases (STDs), and the psychological effects it may have on you in marriage.

BALANCE

Maturity implies balance. Balance is another word that differentiates a child from a man. For instance when you are a child, you could not balance properly on a bicycle so you rode a tricycle. But as an adult you ride a bicycle.

Balance is very important in any man's life as it makes you cautious of how you spend your time and money, the kind of company you keep and the places you go.

Responsibility also goes hand in hand with balance. It separates men from boys. Children usually don't have purpose so they can spend a whole day playing but maturity comes into play when one knows when to stop. It is a common saying that, "All work and no play, makes jack a doll boy." But I'd like to add, "All play and no work makes jack a poor man". The truth is if you refuse to work, you will always be broke and as a man that is totally unacceptable. Now there is nothing wrong with having fun, but the key is balance. God expects us to achieve balance in everything we do.

"A false balance is abomination to the LORD..."

- Proverbs 11: 1

God hates it when we lack balance in our lives. The Bible makes it clear that balance is essential in life. According to Ecclesiastes there is time for everything.

4 [There is] a time to weep, and a time to laugh; a time to mourn, and a time to dance; 5 a time to cast away stones, and a time to gather stones together; a time to embrace and a time to refrain from embracing; 6 a time to get and a time to lose; a time to keep and a time to cast away; 7 a time to rend and a time to sew; a time to keep silence and a time to speak."
-Ecclesiastes 3:4-7

CONTROL

"He that hath no rule over his own spirit is like a city that is broken down, and without walls".
- Proverbs 25:28

"He that is slow to anger is better than the mighty; and he that ruleth (or control) his spirit than he that taketh a city".
- Proverbs 16:32

Learning to control yourself is a major factor in maturity. Self-control is a major issue in marriage. When a person lacks self control, it will only get worse in marriage. For instance, if a man can slap his fiancée, he will have no problem beating her up when they eventually get married. You must learn self-control in little things or else you will not be able to handle major issues in marriage.

You must sit down and ask yourself honestly, "Do I have self-control?" "Can I control my anger, envy, bitterness, rage, malice, and unforgiveness?" "The person I am planning to marry, can he or she control him or her self?"

Some men fall in love with women purely on how beautiful she looks, without even getting to know the person. While some women fall in love with a man just because of his profession, position, or possession. They fall in love with total strangers. This is a fruit of lack of emotional control.

In the kingdom of God, we do not fall in love, we grow in love. If you have been falling in love, get up and get a hold on yourself. The bible says, *"The righteous man may fall seven times but rises up again."*

(Proverbs 24:16). So no matter how many times you have fallen in love, you can get up and get a grip on yourself.

It is very important that you know a person well before you can love that person. The most important thing is the character of the person and not his or her charisma. Charisma may attract you to the person but it would take character to maintain or manage a relationship or marriage. You must always remember that all that glitters is not gold. Some people have beauty without brains. Some people are attractive without character. You should ask yourself if that is the kind of person you want to be involved with.

Incidentally, most times the people that are going to be the most important in your life are people you may not be attracted to at first. After a while, you may start to notice some things about them such as their good character, meekness, and their commitment to God among other things that you will discover over time. That's the beauty of relationships. It's those things that you discover over time that will draw you closer to the person and make you have a stronger bond.

If you keep yearning for total strangers, you have to be careful because you may end up getting involved with an armed robber, a liar, fraud or even an occultist. The church is a place for every kind of person. All kinds of people come with different motives, so the mere fact that you see a brother in church is not enough reason to start desiring him without actually getting to know him first or getting any information about him. Even Jesus said he came for the lost and the sinners. Therefore, the church is a hospital. As Jesus puts it "only the sick needs a physician". For all you know that man you are so attracted to may just be pretending to be a saint while in actual sense he is very far from being that.

Ladies, you must learn to control your emotions. Since women are emotional beings, it is easy to get carried away by feelings thereby making wrong decisions. You must put your emotions under check.

Men, you on the other hand must control your hormones.

SELF DENIAL

Self-denial, which is another sign of maturity, implies the ability to delay gratification. It means the ability to forfeit immediate pleasure for future gain or honour.

Let us consider the story of Esau and Jacob in the bible with practical references to Gen 25:29-33,

29. "and Jacob sod pottage: and Esau came from the field and he was faint.
30. And Esau said to Jacob, feed me, I pray thee, with that same red pottage; for I am faint: therefore was his name called Edom.
31. And Jacob said; sell me this day thy birth right.
32. And Esau said; behold, I am at the point to did [He could not delay gratification]: *and what profit shall this birthright do to me?*
33. And Jacob said, swear to me this day; and he swore unto him: and sold his birthright unto Jacob."

Esau lost his birthright (a long-term benefit) for short satisfaction or pleasure just because he could not control himself. Anyone that cannot delay gratification can throw away a long-term relationship for short-lived pleasure. They can trade anything to satisfy their desire. Their best word is NOW. They do not think of future consequences.

For instance, anyone who asks for sex outside marriage and cannot take no for an answer, is not really ready for the long-term commitment of marriage. He wants what he can get now and will most likely be unfaithful in marriage. Such a person will be dangerous because he cannot delay pleasure. He has urges like everyone else but refuses to deny himself of the pleasure of sex till the right time. He is simply an adulterer in the making. Because he cannot control himself, he will sleep with anyone who will let him, even his wife's sister.

However, I don't put all the blame on the man. Some women encourage men to be promiscuous. If a man demands for sex before marriage and threatens to leave if he doesn't get it, they have sex with the man in a bid to keep him. The truth is, it doesn't matter if you succumb under the pressure of losing him or not, when he can get what he wants with you, he will probably try to get it again from someone else and might even end up dumping you. He must learn to control himself. If a person cannot sacrifice immediate pleasure for long-term benefit, that person is like a time bomb the relationship can explode in your face at any time. It is absolutely unthinkable to pair up with such a person.

DIFFERENT AREAS OF MATURITY

Maturity must be seen in different areas of a person's life before (s)he can be considered eligible for marriage. These are the areas in which you must exhibit maturity before you can handle the issues of relationship or marriage.

PHYSICAL MATURITY

The Bible never gave any specific age range for marriage but the socio-culture and socioeconomic standard of a particular society go a long way in determining the appropriate age for courtship or marriage. In this part of the world, it is advisable for ladies to be at least 20 years old and the men at least 24 years old.

Some people have been known to marry at much younger ages but it is unadvisable to go into an intimate relationship as a teenager. At this stage of your life, a lot of things are changing about you and you will just have started discovering things about yourself. It will be advisable to take time to grow and discover yourself. As you grow older, you will get more exposed and your values will change. Your opinions will change a great deal as well. So you should spend those years discovering and building yourself in every way you can.

MENTAL MATURITY

A mature person must exhibit that he possesses a mind of his own. He must be creative and intelligent. He must be able to make important decisions on his own without depending on his parents or friends.

He must be able to think things through and make quality decisions. It is an immature man that thinks he must ask his mothers opinion before making decisions. He even puts his mother before his wife. I've even seen men with children of their own behave with such immaturity. I am not saying you should not seek advice when necessary but the buck ends with you. Be the man God has called you to be. A matured man must be able to take responsibility for his life and actions without blaming friends, family and society for whatever situation he finds himself.

One of the most common things people say is "I don't want to marry her but my father or my pastor made me do it." That is the height of irresponsibility! Adam made a similar statement and God punished him for it. Only when you take responsibility for your decisions can you truly say you are mentally prepared for marriage. You will be expected to make life-changing decisions in marriage and you shall take responsibility for them.

You must also realize that the anointing is not equal to wisdom. The anointing is an empowerment to serve; wisdom is what you use in making decisions in your daily life. The anointing is not and cannot be a substitute for common knowledge. You need practical experiences to be able to handle real issues. That's why the bible says,

"Wisdom is the principal thing: therefore get wisdom; and with all thy getting, get understanding".
-Proverbs 4:7

Mental maturity is simply applying of wisdom in handling everyday affairs.

SOCIAL MATURITY
This is another major area in which people must exhibit maturity in other to be considered ready for marriage. It is important that you show good communication and people skills. Some people have problem relating with others in public. They are either too shy or too forward. Others simply needs to learn

simple etiquette, how to eat, how to speak, how to act and relate with others in public. You must learn when and how to use words around people. Learn the power behind words like, "thank you", "please" and "excuse me". You will need these words and the maturity it takes to use them in marriage or relationship. Relating with people or possessing people skills will also help when dealing with in-laws.

FINANCIAL MATURITY
A regular source of income is very important in any man's life before he can ever think of settling down. If he still collects pocket money from his parents, he lacks financial maturity and is definitely not ready for marriage. A man must be able to make, manage and multiply money. It is very dangerous to think of settling down with a man who is always begging, borrowing and broke.

He must be able to earn a living for himself. Even when no one gives him a job, he should be able to create one. Many able-bodied men sit at home doing nothing with the excuse that they are planning to travel out of the country. It's okay to travel if it's God's will for you but while you are waiting, find something to do. The Bible says he that does not work should not eat. So there is no excuse for idleness.

Financial maturity is not just about having money. Some people are spendthrifts. They have no control over how they spend money. They are compulsive shoppers and squanderers.

Proverbs 21:17 says,
"He that loveth pleasure shall be a poor man: He that loveth wine and oil shall not be rich."

You should be mature enough to handle decisions about money especially where they involve sharing it with someone else. Monetary issues in marriage involve two people who are mature financially. The Bible says in 1 Timothy 5:8,

"But if any provide not for his own, and especially for those of his house hold, he

hath denied the faith, and is worse than an infidel".

The above scripture says, 'if any...' which implies that the Bible is not referring to men alone as is commonly believed. Infact in verse 16 it says clearly, "if any man or woman..." so financial responsibility is not for men alone.

Therefore, financial maturity is a very important characteristic that must be exhibited by Christians whether male or female, married or single.

SPIRITUAL MATURITY

Spiritual maturity is one area that cannot be compromised in marriage. Many people think that when you can speak in tongues or pray for long hours that you are spiritually mature. The volumes of scriptures that they can quote deceive themselves and others. The truth is that even if you can raise the dead when you walk by, you are not necessarily spiritually mature. Spiritual maturity is not measured by the gifts of the spirit but by the fruit of the spirit.

"Wherefore by their fruit ye shall know them".

-Matthew 7:20

The gifts of the Spirit are spiritual manifestations that occur from time to time in a believer as the Holy Spirit wills.

7. But the manifestation of the Spirit is given to every man to profit withal.
8. For to one is given by the spirit... (And it goes on to mention the 9 gifts of the spirit)
11. But all these worketh that one and the same Spirit dividing to everyman severally as he will.

-1corinthians 12:7, 8 &11

The fruit of the Spirit on the other hand, are our personal responsibility. It is not something we expect God to do. It is the character and conduct expected of us as Christians and it should reflect in our daily living.

"22. But the fruit of the Spirit is love, joy, peace, longsuffering, gentleness, goodness, faith.
23. Meekness, temperance: against such there is no law.

-*Galatians 5: 22-23*

Spiritual maturity also involves having an intimate relationship with God, being led by his spirit and recognizing his voice.

"For as many as are led by the spirit of God, they are the sons of a God."

- Romans 8:14

Some Christians wait till they have to make major decisions like marriage before seeking God's will (leading and direction). They have never sought God on any other issue in their life prior to this. Suddenly, they expect to hear God concerning a life partner. God won't lead you any differently from how he has been leading you in the past. That is, if you have ever been led by Him before. If you have never been led of God in the past, it is risky to wake up one day and claim to have heard God concerning a life partner.

Though maturity is a function of wisdom, responsibility and exposure, information cannot be substituted for time. True maturity takes time. You may be informed through books and tapes and still not be matured. It takes time to grow up. You must take your time. You must be matured before getting involved.

CHAPTER FIVE

DO YOU KNOW YOUR PURPOSE?

"Where there is no vision, the people perish ..."

-proverbs 2:18 a

Your purpose in life affects every decision you make; the way you talk, the people you associate with, the places you go, the things that interest you, as well as your general attitude towards life.

Purpose is important. It is your God-given vision, goal, dream, and aspiration or chosen career. Purpose is knowing where you are headed in life. Since marriage is a major part of life, it is therefore important that you know your destination in life before choosing a partner, you can be sure you are headed in the same direction. You must be sure of your purpose in life so you can make the right choice of who will help in achieving that purpose. This is not a farfetched principle even God gave Adam work to do before he gave him a wife.

15." And the Lord God took the man and put him into the Garden of Eden to dress and keep it. **(God gave him a job, a purpose or an Assignment)**

18. And the Lord God said it is not good that the man should be alone; I will make him a helpmeet **(a wife, adequate, qualified, suitable and adaptable)** *for him* **(and his assignment)."**

-Genesis 2:15&18

God did not just give him a wife; he gave him a helper, a wife adequate or qualified to help him with his purpose or his job. You have to know your purpose in life before you can find someone who is suitable to help you achieve that purpose.

You are not ready for courtship or marriage until you have discovered the purpose for your life. Your partner's purpose must align with yours. You must be heading in the same direction. The Bible says in Amos 3:3,

"Can two walk together, except they be agreed?"

If you don't have purpose, how will you know if two of you agree?
There are certain questions you must ask yourself:
Do I know my purpose in life?
Does my partner know her purpose?
Do our purposes align?
The answer to these questions must be in the affirmative for you to propose to a lady. It is dangerous to propose to a lady without knowing which way she is headed.

KNOW YOUR PURPOSE IN LIFE BEFORE GETTING A PARTNER FOR LIFE.

Your purpose in life should determine your choice of a life partner. For instance, if your assignment is to sell products from door to door, and you are asked to pick a partner, you will obviously not pick a shy person. Let me paint a clearer picture, for instance, two men are purposing to you and they are both called Michael. One is Michael Jackson and the other Michael Tyson. Now, let's say that your purpose is to build a word-class, internationally recognized choir with the goal of winning a Grammy. Who would you pick as a husband? Definitely Michael Jackson! The fact that he is known all over the world with a lot of awards and the prospect of him coming into the studio to help with the rehearsals will attract the kind of people you need. Your purpose in life directly affects your choice of partner in life.

The person you choose as a life partner must fit into the big picture of your life. Don't just marry based on what you are right now, but on where you are going.

Some people have gotten married not knowing that they will later become public figures and will always be in the limelight. When their status changed, they suddenly realized that the wife they married then was no longer suitable for the life they now lived. That's the reason some of the presidents and top officials in this part of the world marry many other wives, presenting the suitable one as the first lady, when in actual fact she is the third lady.

I must also say this, for those who are called to a life of ministry; it is not enough to know you are called into the ministry. You must know exactly what area of the ministry and what kind, as this will determine your choice of partner. For example, the wife of a pastor will be different from the wife of an evangelist though they are both ministers.

AVOID DIVISION

The word DIVISION is a combination of two words: 'DI and 'VISION'. DI means two, while 'VISION' stands for purpose. When we have two visions, we have division.
You can have division in marriage when two of you have separate visions.

Take the case of an American preacher I once heard of who had to divorce his wife. After many years of marriage, she woke up one morning saying she has just discovered she was called to be a missionary to Africa. Since the man was called to be a preacher in America and she a missionary in Africa, this brought division, two separate visions into the marriage. They had to go their separate ways.

The issue of division has led to the dissolution of many marriages. Usually the couples do not discuss and settle the issue of purpose before getting married. As a pastor, I have a purpose for my life, so I need a qualified or adequate partner, someone suitable and adaptable (a helpmeet). I had to be particular about my choice. It will be unwise to choose a helper without having a purpose or knowing what you need help for. That is why as a pastor, I allowed my purpose determine the kind of wife I married.

I am not saying there was any thing wrong with the other women I have met. I am just saying that some of them were not just cut out to be pastor's wives. They may be suitable for businessmen, career people or professionals in other areas but they are not for people called to ministry like pastors.

A pastor's wife should be a mother, not just to her children but also to her church. She must love God, her husband and the people. She must love God first or else she will be selfish, desiring to keep her husband away from the work and the people. The life of a pastor is sacrificial too; sacrifice her time, money and her husband.

Personally, I couldn't have married a wife that frets over hearsay. As a pastor's wife, you must be ready to love a public life. People will constantly misunderstand and talk about you, your husband and your ministry. People have said all kind of things about me but I don't let that border me. My only response to my critics is to succeed, and success has such an undeniable voice!

GET A LIFE!
"If you don't have a purpose for living, you are not fit to live".
 Martin Luther King.

You must get a life. You must have something you are living for other than marriage. You must have things you are passionate about; things that satisfy your soul... don't just centre your life on your partner (s)he can't be all things to you. Take time to discover your purpose. Marriage should not be your ultimate goal in life. Marriage itself is not an end but a means to an end. FULFILLMENT!!!

SO REMEMBER YOU NEED A PURPOSE FOR LIFE BEFORE CHOOSING A PARTNER FOR LIFE.

CHAPTER SIX

ARE YOU SINGLE?

"And ye are complete in him."
-Colossians 2:10a

Being single is not a sin. It is not something to be ashamed of. Some single people feel inferior, lonely, and unwanted. They feel like something must be wrong with them simply because they do not have a partner. There is nothing wrong with being single. As a matter of fact, you should be single before you get married.

Myles Munroe once said, "The omelette is only as good as the egg it is made from." This is the same as saying:

"Every marriage is only as good as the two individuals involved." This means that if two junkies get married, nothing but junk can come out of that marriage.

Being single is not a curse. It merely means to be COMPLETE, which connotes UNIQUE, SEPARATE and WHOLE.

BE UNIQUE
God is so interested in uniqueness that no two people have the same composition. We all have different biological and physical attributes; different finger prints, different DNA and so on. You must stop trying to be like someone else.

As a pastor, I cannot risk loosing my identity trying to be like other pastors. I don't try to talk like Bishop T.D Jakes, or Bishop David Oyedepo. These people stand out by being themselves. I want to preach as good as they do and have results like them or even better, but I don't want to be any of them. I want to be me and succeed as me and at being me.

Don't loose your identity or uniqueness trying to be someone else. There is nothing wrong with trying to be LIKE someone else, that is, trying to emulate someone's success or being inspired by someone else but you must NEVER try to be that person. Be yourself. Be unique.

When you try to be someone else, you just become a signpost telling people about the original. The most you can ever achieve trying to be someone else is second best. God created you an original, don't die a copy. Believe in yourself. Enjoy being you. Be satisfied with being you.

I've often heard my pastor, Reverend Femi Oduwole, how amazingly dissatisfied people are in the world today. And it is absolutely true.
He often says:
"The short are wearing heels to appear taller, while the tall are wearing flat shoes to appear shorter.
The light skinned are tanning to look darker, while the black skinned are bleaching to look lighter.

Boys apply methylated spirit to grow beards to look older, while men shave theirs to look younger.

Workers dress in jeans to look like students, while students dress corporate to look like workers.

Be yourself but keep improving on yourself. Some people even over do it by going as far as not only copying how people talk or act, even their hairstyles and dress styles. Don't lose your identity for any reason. BE UNIQUE.

BE SEPARATE

God created us as separate individuals. He created us ALONE- alone means 'All in one'. Which means you have all you need in you to live a fulfilled life? Fulfilment comes from within, not from people. Don't try to attach yourself to anyone forcefully. Some people make comments such as,

"If I don't marry him or her, my life is shattered."

Honey, your life got shattered long before that!

Until you can get to the point when you can look at anyone in the eye, whether a pastor or miss world, and say with conviction, "I know who I am and I know my worth. I don't need anyone to validate me". Then, you are not yet separate. You need to exhibit that level of good self-esteem. Yes, I know that you may need to work on improving yourself but you must know your worth.

Many people have entered into slavery in the name of marriage. They say to themselves, "This man is everything and I am a nobody, if I don't marry him, I am finished."

No one should intimidate you. You are too loaded for that. If someone says no to you (and you are sure that you have spent time improving yourself) it may simply means that (s)he cannot discern a good product when (s)he sees one and simply has bad taste. That person is not the right person for you.

Build yourself up to the point where no one can make you feel inferior. Don't leave your self-esteem in the hands of men. Don't base yourself esteem on people's opinion of you. Their opinion may vary and change from time to time. Don't expect people to always believe in you or agree with everything you do. Some people will do anything to get acceptance. They just want everyone to like them even if it means displeasing God and themselves. Joyce Meyer calls it approval addiction.

Well, I have news for you honey, everyone cannot like you. The Bible says 'woe unto you if all men speak well of you'. You are created to please God and not people. Remember we are created for his pleasure.

On the other hand, don't put people down just to feel good. As is often said, *just because you criticize the weeds in your brother's garden doesn't keep them from growing in yours.* A good self-esteem is not about feeling superior to others; it is about feeling good about yourself. You must also learn not to base your self-esteem on fickle things. For instance, if your self-esteem is based on your looks, you will definitely meet someone who is more beautiful than you are. Just learn to feel good about yourself without making unnecessary comparisons. Feel good about who you are, beautify and develop yourself. Human beings are made different on purpose so be your own distinct and separate person. You have only one attempt at life, make the most of it.

BE WHOLE

A lot of people are not whole or complete. They have been broken, battered and shattered. Some people have had terrible past lives and refuse to let God heal them. The past is the past. Stop putting blame on the past and your past experiences. No matter what happened then, you can put it all behind you and start living the now. No matter what you've been through, no matter what people have done to you, no matter what your parents did to you, you can start again.

Even if you were raped, now that you are born again, Christ is in you and he is the hope of glory. God can heal that hurt. Open your heart and be healed. Every one has been through one bad experience or the other so yours is not an excuse to remain angry, bitter and depressed. The past is PAST; now move on and be healed by the word. Also, you must never get married to a person who is not whole because when things go wrong (s)he will always have the past as an excuse while refusing to change. If you don't deal with your past it will affect your marriage.

HURTING PEOPLE HURT PEOPLE

Just like in the case of Joyce Meyer, who had an abusive childhood that left her angry, bitter and hurt. She carried her hurting past into her marriage, which almost ruined it until she received healing from Christ. She forgave her father, (you have no right to hold on to anyone's sins when God has forgiven your own) who is now saved. Christ can heal you too. He can heal you physically, spiritually and emotionally.

This is one of the major reasons why it is always advisable for victims of broken relationship to take time off to get healed emotionally (to be whole) before getting into another relationship. However, most people, rather than take time to evaluate the previous relationship to discover where they missed it, just jump into another relationship. They usually end up taking their pain or anger (from the last relationship) out on their new partner consciously or unconsciously because the truth is that, hurting people hurt people. Don't stay broken, battered and shattered. Get healed and be made whole.

Even if you've been through a lot of rejection and you feel no one cares or no one loves you, I have good news for you. God loves you. Jesus loves you. They can be the father or the mother you never had, the friends that you need. The Bible says in Psalm 27:10[NKJV]

"When my father and mother forsake me; then the Lord will take care of me".

The truth is, Jesus can be anything you want him to be for you. You will have all the love and affection that you yearn for. God's love is constant, unconditional and ever sure. He said he will never leave or forsake you (Hebrews 13:5). So embrace that love and receive wholeness. You need it to be complete. That's what it means to be SINGLE.

Be Unique. Be Separate. Be Whole... Be COMPLETE!!!

CHAPTER SEVEN

WHERE IS GOD IN ALL OF THESE?

"4...And he answered and said unto them, have you not read, that he which made them at the beginning made them male and female,

5. And said for this cause shall a man leave his father and mother, and shall cleave to his wife and they twain shall be one flesh?

6. Wherefore they are no more twain but one flesh. What therefore God hath joined together let no man put asunder."

- Matthew 19:4-6

God is not only the originator of marriage, but also its sustainer. There is no guarantee that your marriage will work out if it is not centred on God. It is what he upholds that stays together.

"...upholding all things by the word of His power".

-Hebrews 1:3

God should have first place in your individual lives. This should tell you that as a believer, marrying an unbeliever is completely out of the question. You have no business proposing to an unbeliever or agreeing to marry one.

14." Be ye not unequally yoked together with unbelievers; for what fellowship has righteousness with unrighteousness? And what communion hath light with darkness? 15. And what concord hath Christ with Belial? Or what part hath he that believeth with an infidel?

16. And what agreement hath the temple of God with idols? For ye are the temple of the living God: as God hath said, I will dwell in them and walk in them, and I will be their God and they will be my people.

17. Wherefore come out from among them and be ye separate saith the Lord, and touch not the unclean thing; and I will receive you 18. And will be a father unto you and ye shall be my sons and daughters saith the Lord Almighty."

-2 Corinthians 6:14-18

Commitment is a major issue in marriage. You must however take note of the fact that if someone cannot commit himself to the Almighty God, His creator, the one who sent His only son –Jesus to die for him, then there is absolutely no way that same person can be committed to you.

You must also take the time to ask yourself, "Where is God in my life?" before you start looking for a partner. Don't consider someone when you cannot see God as a priority in the person's life. It's not even enough for the person to be born again. (S)he must be committed to obeying God. It's not just about being an usher, chorister, or even a pastor. People have different reasons for doing things. A chorister may sing in church because (s)he has a talent for singing and may not really be committed to God. Find out the motive behind what you do or what the person you want to marry does before taking the decision to get married or even enter into a relationship.

You would be amazed at how many people are after the glory and not necessarily after God. Some people just want to be pastors because they like the pastoral life assuming that it is all about the money and glory.

I have come in contact with people who say things like, "I am called to be a world evangelist. I have combined anointing of Billy Graham and Reinhard Bonnke. I want to win souls for God".

When I ask them, "what is your motive? Is it for the glory or do you have a heart for souls?"

They reply with indignation, "I have a heart for souls!"
Then I ask them," How many souls have you won around you in your neighbourhood?"

"Actually... I ...I" they begin to stutter. In cases like these, it is obvious that the person is after the glory.

You really want to be a world evangelist and you have not won souls around you? Your neighbours are unbelievers. Your mother is going straight to hell and you are just sitting there eating her food? Stop fooling yourself!

Some others will say, "I want to be a kingdom financier. I have passion for the kingdom of God." But whenever the opportunity arises to give financially, they come up with all kinds of excuses. There is a price you must pay in everything you do in life. These people aren't willing to pay the price. They are not committed to God or the things of God.

You really must be wise when it comes to choosing a life partner. Take your time. Study people. Look out for spiritual qualities or the fruits of the spirit. Look out for that person with a meek and quiet spirit, with sound character who is willing to obey God no matter the cost. Don't be moved by physical appearance and qualities. Remember that all that glitters is not gold. The Bible says in Proverbs 31:30,

"Favour (charm) is deceitful, and beauty is vain but a woman who fears the Lord, she shall be praised."

DON'T MARRY A MAN OR WOMAN WHO LOVES YOU MORE THAN (S)HE LOVES GOD

In marriage there will be times when your spouse will be tempted to sin against you. However, if (s)he loves God more than (s)he loves you, the fear of God will put him or her in check. Just like in the case of Portiphar's wife, when his master's wife was making passes at him, Joseph said, "How can I do this thing and sin against my God?"

7. "And it came to pass after these things that his master's wife cast her eyes upon Joseph, and she said, lie with me.
8. But he refused and said unto his master's wife, behold my master wotteth not what is

with me in the house, and he hath committed all that he hath to my hand.

9.   There is none greater in the house than I: neither hath he kept back anything from me but thee, because thou art wife: how then can I do these great wickedness, and sin against God?

10. and it came to pass, as she spake to Joseph day by day, that he hearkened not unto her, to lie by her, or to be with her.

-Genesis 39:7-10

It wasn't about Portiphar. Joseph feared and loved God more than anything else. Portiphar wouldn't have known but he couldn't just find it in himself to displease God. This is the reason why you must marry someone who loves and reverence God more than he loves you. There will be times the person may be tempted to sin against you, because he loves God, he will not do it. On the other hand, if he loves you more than he loves God he will say to himself, "she won't know, let me just do it." He will do it and keep it secret; just like Portiphar's wife was tempted to lie with Joseph. As she did not fear God and believed her husband wouldn't know. She had nothing to restrain her from her adulterous desire.

There will also be times your partner will offend you, probably even unknowingly, but if you fear and love God, you will not act contrary to God's word. For instance , if your wife is rude to you and your natural instinct is to slap her and teach her a lesson, because you fear God and know his word, "Husbands love your wives…" you will not do it. That's one of the reasons I like it when people make statements like, "If not for God…" that's a good statement. If it is because of God that you wont do something wrong, that's good.

"For this is commendable if because of conscience toward God one endure grief, suffering wrongfully."
-1 pet 2: 19[NKJV]

Finally, if your spouse loves God more than he loves you, he will respect and honour you because of God.

LET GOD BE THE UMPIRE

Another advantage of making God the centre of your lives is that God becomes the umpire of your marriage. God's word acts as the umpire maintaining law and order just as a referee or an umpire maintain law and order in the football match and makes sure nobody goes against the rules; and even when a player breaks the rule, the referee cautions him appropriately and restores order to the game. In the same way Gods word becomes the standard maintaining law and order in your marriage.

Likewise, ye husbands dwell with them according to knowledge, giving honour unto the wife as unto the weaker vessel, and as being heirs together of the grace of life: that your prayers be not hindered.

-1 pet 3:7

Make God your foundation. Let God have his place in your life. He will help you build a successful marriage.

"For every house is builded by some man: but he that built all things is God."

- Hebrews 3:4

Some people are looking for a perfect spouse. Someone they can trust and rely on, but the truth is, no one is perfect. We are all prone to making mistakes. Trusting God is the only way to lasting peace in your life and marriage.

CHAPTER EIGHT

IS PREPARATION REALLY NECESSARY?

1. Then shall the kingdom of heaven be likened unto ten virgins, which took their lamps, and went forth to meet the bridegroom.
2. And five of them were wise and five were foolish.
3. They that were foolish took their lamps, and took no oil with them.
4. But the wise took oil in their vessels with their lamps.
5. While the bridegroom tarried, they all slumbered and slept.

6. *and at mid night, there was a cry made, behold the bridegroom cometh; go ye out to meet him.*

7. *Then all those virgins arose and trimmed their lamps.*

8. *and the foolish said unto the wise, give us of your oil; for our lamps are gone out.*

9. *But the wise answered, saying, not so; lest there be not enough for us and you: but go ye rather to them that sell, and buy for yourselves.*

10. *And while they went to buy, the bridegroom came; and they that were ready went in with him to the marriage: and the door was shut.*

11. *Afterwards came also the other virgins, Lord, Lord, open to us.*

12. *But he answered and said, verily I say unto you, I know you not.*

13. *Watch therefore: for ye know neither the day nor hour where in the son of man cometh.*

-Matthew 25: 1-3

In life, most people hope for the best they can get, but the wise one don't only hope, they do all that is within their power to enhance their chances of getting it.

A wise man once said, proper preparation prevents poor performance. Life has always shown that opportunity favours the prepared man. Some people just sit and assume that when it's time to get married or get into courtship; they will just automatically know what to do. To truly make the most of opportunity in life you will really need to be prepared for it. It is foolish to assume you will automatically be ready when the time for you to be married comes without taking the time to prepare yourself for it.

In the parable above, the five foolish virgins missed their opportunity because they were not prepared when the bridegroom came. They had no oil in their lamps and they knew it but did nothing about it till the last minute. The five wise ones that were prepared made the most of the opportunity when it arose.

That is exactly what most people do. They know they want to get married or they are getting closer to an age where they are eligible for marriage, but they do nothing to prepare themselves and enhance their chances of having the best kind of marriage. They just wait till the last moment like the foolish virgins, before they start preparing; and they foolishly expect to get the best kind of partner. Why don't you think about it as well, if you have to choose between a novice who knows nothing about marriage, still complains about his/her past, has no vision or direction and is financially unstable and someone who is mature, properly informed about his or her role in marriage, who has the right perspective about marriage and is financially stable, who would you pick?

There are even instances where people that were engaged, who thought they were home free have lost their partners to someone who was more prepared than they were for marriage.

A MORE HONOURABLE MAN OR WOMAN

8." When thou art bidden of any man to a wedding, sit not thou in the highest room; lest a MORE HONOURABLE MAN (or WOMAN) than thou be bidden of him;
9. And he that bade thee and he come and say to thee give this man place; and thou begin with shame to take the lowest room."
-Luke 14:8-9

The above scripture paints a picture of what will happen to a person who is unprepared. When a more prepared (more honourable) one comes on the scene he will be side lined. The fact that you are engaged to a particular person presently does not guarantee you anything. If you keep refusing to add value to your life or you don't do things to ensure that you maintain your position, when a more honourable man or woman someone who is physically, spiritually, emotionally, and financially mature comes , (s)he will naturally displace you irrespective of how long you've been there or how much you've invested. I must emphasis here that both the one who left for someone else and the one who displaced the other person are not wicked or heartless, it just so happens that everyone wants the best they can get. Opportunity really does favour the prepared man.

CAN I REALLY GET MY HEART DESIRE?
During one of our seminars, a young lady once approached me with this question. She said, "Most of the guys that approach me are not my heart desire. The kind of men that I like never proposes. Is it that the right guy has not come my way? I can't afford to marry someone I don't love."

You see, pertaining to her question, the truth is that, it seems men are at an advantage because they can go for what they want but as a lady every kind of person can approach you. It is now up to you to pick the most suitable for you. Now if you want to attract the right kind of people, you must find out what they like or desire in a spouse. For instance, if you want to marry a pastor, find out what they like or desire in a wife they would most likely want a woman who is spiritual, well mannered, meek and peaceful, amongst other things. The question you should ask yourself is, "If I were to be a pastor, would I marry me?" if the answer is 'no', then you need to work on yourself till you become the kind of person that attracts pastors.

This principle applies to whatever kind of person you want, be it a businessman, a professional, or a career person. It also applies in the area of the person's qualities, standard and so on. You must adjust accordingly. Work on yourself, your values. As a believer, if you are attracting only unbelievers, then something is wrong some where. Improve your standards; improve yourself continually till you measure up to what you want to be.

As long as your desires are not unscriptural and unrealistic; hold on to them and God will grant you the desires of your heart. You must also be sensitive because your ideal partner will most likely come in potential form and it will be up to you to help him or her release and maximize their potentials.

However, be careful not to keep trying to measure up to any man or woman's unrealistic standards because there are some gifts, talents, or qualities you don't have and would never have. If the person cannot do without them, this should just tell you that the person is not meant for you.

WHAT WILL BE WILL BE

Some people have the philosophy that, what is mine will surely come to me no matter what I do or don't do or what's gonna be is gonna be and there is nothing you can do about it. This belief or philosophy is not only wrong but quite foolish and unrealistic.

This is just like saying or believing that without attending lectures or reading for exams, if you are meant to pass the exams, you will. Let's also consider that there was an opportunity at your place of work for a promotion or even that your company was laying off workers, would you go to work once in a week and believe that what's meant to be will be? Won't you increase your performance at work and do everything within your power to get the promotion or keep your job?

The truth about life is that nothing just happens. People make them happen. There must be at least some kind of input before you can expect to get your desired result. So it is not what's gonna be is gonna be but what you make happen will be!

YOU NEED TO RECIEVE JESUS AS LORD!!!

This book is written purely for believers and there is no guarantee that if adhered to strictly as an unbeliever that it will bring the desire results.

So for the principles in this book to work, you must surrender your life to Christ. If you are willing to do this, say this prayer from your heart:

Dear Heavenly Father, I come to you as I am.
Help me Lord, I can't help myself. Deliver me
from the power of sin and satan and
translate me to kingdom of your dear Son
Jesus.
I believe according to Romans 10: 9-10 that
died for me and arose on the third day. I

confess you today as my Lord and Saviour.

*Thank you Lord for I now know that I am
Born again and fit for heaven.*

Made in the USA
Middletown, DE
10 June 2024

55537440R00066